IT'S GREAT TO BE ME

Daily Affirmations for Children

Written by
Melissa Ahonen

Illustrated by
Daria Shamolina

IT'S GREAT TO BE ME

Published by Dandelion Dreams Publishing (Melissa Ahonen, LLC)
www.melissaahonen.com
Lincoln, ND

Text and Illustration Copyright 2021: Melissa Ahonen. All rights reserved.
2nd Edition
Edited by: Myriah C. Boudreaux

All rights reserved. No portion of this book may be reproduced or transmitted in any form or by any means, electronic or mechanical, including photocopying, recording, or any information storage and retrieval system, without written permission from the author, except by reviewer who may quote passages in a review.

Library of Congress Control Number: 2021920051

ISBN: 978-1-7377121-1-4 (hardcover)
978-1-7377121-0-7 (paperback)

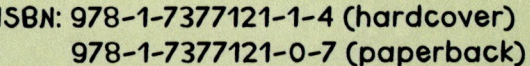

All inquiries of this book can be sent to the
author at melissa@melissaahonen.com.
For more information or to book an event,
please visit www.melissaahonen.com

This book is printed in the United States of America.

To Easton and Aspen: Thank you for pushing me to be the mom I am today. I hope you know how amazing you both are, and you can change the world.

To Jim: Thank you for being my biggest support and letting me chase my dreams and check off my bucket list one by one.

To my mom: Thank you for teaching me from a young age not to dull my light because others choose to live in darkness. You have shown me that raising strong, confident children who believe in themselves is the best thing a mom can do for her kids.

To my sisters: Thank you for being my sounding boards and my hype team. I've got your backs, you've got mine.

I love you all.

It's good to remind yourself, "I am great!"
So, let's not hesitate.
You are special just being you.
Believe. That's all you need to do.

Repeat each of these after me,
and you will soon see
that you are exactly all you are saying and more.
Believe it, and you will soar.

I AM STRONG!

I know I can think things through
when figuring out the right thing to do.
Some choices are hard, yet others are easy to make,
like choosing which cookies to help Mom bake!
I AM STRONG!

I AM EXCELLENT!

Deep down inside and all throughout,
I know I'm not perfect, but I am excellent, no doubt.
From my clusters of freckles to my silly, crooked grin.
Although I may have lost, I still cheer my brother's win.
I AM EXCELLENT!

I AM CONFIDENT!

I believe in myself every day.
I can achieve anything I say.
Like the time I ran a race,
and I took first place!
I AM CONFIDENT!

I AM UNIQUE!

Each person is different in their own special way,
and that is more than just okay!
From head to toe, we are each one of a kind!
No one is exactly like me that you will find.
I AM UNIQUE!

I AM SMART!

I can do anything I put my mind to,
even if it's hard to do.
Someday, I can invent something new.
There's no limit to what I can do.
I AM SMART!

I AM BRAVE!

I can face things that are serious

or just a little curious.

I accept challenges – new, tough, or scary.

I can even confront that monster who looks rather hairy.

I AM BRAVE!

I AM GRATEFUL!

I am thankful for all the good I can find.
Blessings big and small. People who are kind.
I love our family and our dog,
who likes when I take him for a jog.
I AM GRATEFUL!

I AM TALENTED!

There are so many things that I can do,
from riding my bike to playing a kazoo.
I can even juggle different balls
without ever letting them fall.
I AM TALENTED!

I AM IMAGINATIVE!

I will dream and reach for the stars.
For me, there is no dream too big or too far.
I can change the world one day,
and I will start dreaming big today.
I AM IMAGINATIVE!

I AM KIND!

I help others when they are in need.
Kindness involves doing good deeds,
like lending a hand when someone gets hurt
or helping plant gardens in the dirt.
I AM KIND!

IT'S GREAT TO BE ME!
I am strong, excellent, confident, unique and smart,
brave, grateful, and talented, with an imaginative and kind heart.
I am grateful and talented as can be.
I am imaginative, dreaming beyond what I can see.
I LOVE MYSELF!

DAILY REFLECTION QUESTIONS

Ask your child a question. Sit quietly and listen to them when they answer you. Having open and honest communication with each other is important to do.

1. What was the best part of your day?
2. What challenge did you have today that might help you grow?
3. How did you help someone today?
4. What are you looking forward to tomorrow?
5. What are you thankful for?
6. If you could have one wish, what would it be?
7. What makes you unique?
8. If there were no obstacles, what would you like to do?

ABOUT THE AUTHOR

Melissa grew up in a creative and imaginative home in Karlsruhe, ND. She spent her days playing outdoors on the farm, where her imagination led her to write endless stories. Her nights were spent hidden beneath her covers, well after bedtime, reading her book by way of flashlight. She now resides in Lincoln, ND, with her husband and their two children.

Melissa draws inspiration from her two children as well as her spirited and mischievous childhood days on the farm. She loves writing about being the best you that you can be and finding the magic in the everyday. When not writing, you will find her chasing after her children, cheering in the hockey rink, and enjoying the outdoors.

Find her online at www.melissaahonen.com

ABOUT THE ILLUSTRATOR

Daria began her illustrating adventure at the age of 14 when she was hired for her first job at a newspaper created by teenagers. She later studied at her local University and began professionally publishing soon after. Daria has llustrated multiple children's books and has a special talent for creating adorable, colorful and bright characters.

Daria resides in the Ukraine with her son, Daniel. He is the greatest love of her life! Becoming a mommy has made all her dreams come true. Daria's favorite activity is going to the zoo with her son and enjoying the many different types of animals together.

Made in the USA
Las Vegas, NV
07 February 2025